The subject of the museum is the recent history of the North-East of England. We tell the story of what life was like here in the years immediately before the First World War. We have been selective. We know that it is impossible to understand totally what life was like for a past generation. The most comprehensive telling is only a partial record of what one generation finds interesting in another. Most museums and history books have traditionally told the stories of richer members of society. Their possessions, records and costumes tend to survive. Working clothes wore out and were thrown away. Records were lost. Victorian cookery books, with their rich multitude of courses, show what the aristocracy or affluent middle classes sometimes ate at special times. Thus, most history is written from the top downwards. Beamish exists to tell history from the bottom upwards. We do not always succeed but we do try.

Beamish is not finished. We have many more projects planned. You will find buildings going up, new displays being fitted. The town area will expand. The tram track is being extended and Pockerley Farm will be developed. Other trades and professions await displays.
We need to say more about politics, trade unionism and the role of women in society. In time, we will bring into the centre of the site a new exhibition area that will make accessible our large photographic archives and library collections. Even when all these projects are in place there will still be much to do. We will continue trying to do it.

What you get from Beamish will be a reflection of what you bring to it. It is easy to believe that the early twentieth-century represents the *good old days*. The period was neither cosy nor rosy. Do not, however, fall into the opposite heresy of believing that these were the *bad old days*, from which late twentieth-century civilisation has rescued us There are lessons to be learned from the generation whose story we tell in this museum.

I am not nostalgic for a time in which a quarter of the population lived in abject poverty unable, in the words of that age, to obtain the minimum necessaries' for existence. I do not want to return to a period in which people lived shorter lives, in which more than half of working-class wives experienced between seven and fifteen pregnancies before reaching the age of forty. I have no longing for an age in which one child in three died at birth or in infancy, in which one person in five could expect a solitary burial from the workhouse, the poor law hospital or the asylum. I note, with thanks, that modern drugs and penicillin have reduced the terrors of measles, diptheria and scarlet fever. I regret that we have other plagues with, as yet, undiscovered remedies.

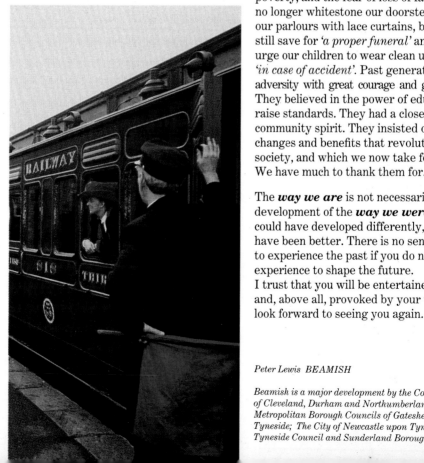

I have a substa[...] [...]iration for the people born in the ear[...] [...] much The men from [...] First World W[...] pounds lighter [...] adversaries. T[...] with their families, the depressions or [...] 1920s and 1930s. They saw the region's large traditional industries fall away. They endured the privations of the 1940s and saw their own children fight and die in a war they thought their own bravery had made impossible.

The thoughts, attitudes and memories of our parents, grandparents and great grand-parents are more deeply engraved in us than we realise. They've passed on to us an essential Englishness, not least a dread of poverty, and the fear of loss of face. We may no longer whitestone our doorsteps or sanctify our parlours with lace curtains, but the old still save for *'a proper funeral'* and we still urge our children to wear clean underwear *'in case of accident'*. Past generations resisted adversity with great courage and good humour. They believed in the power of education to raise standards. They had a closer sense of community spirit. They insisted on social changes and benefits that revolutionised society, and which we now take for granted. We have much to thank them for.

The ***way we are*** is not necessarily a logical development of the ***way we were***. Things could have developed differently, perhaps have been better. There is no sense in seeking to experience the past if you do not use that experience to shape the future.
I trust that you will be entertained, educated and, above all, provoked by your visit. We look forward to seeing you again.

Peter Lewis BEAMISH

Beamish is a major development by the County Councils of Cleveland, Durham and Northumberland; the Metropolitan Borough Councils of Gateshead and South Tyneside; The City of Newcastle upon Tyne, North Tyneside Council and Sunderland Borough Council.

In the nineteenth-century there was a growing need for transport to get people to and from their homes and work. At first horse drawn buses were used, and then, briefly, horse drawn trams. The speed and pulling capacity of a horse is strictly limited. By the 1890s electric tramways were being built in many towns and cities. At their peak there were over 14,000 trams in service in the British Isles. The Beamish fleet consists of four restored trams which operate throughout the year. More are being restored.

Though all of the trams at Beamish are original, the bus is a working replica of a 1913 omnibus. The original was owned and operated by the Gateshead and District Tramways Company, and ran from Chester-le-Street to the Low Fell terminus. The bus is painted in the maroon and cream of the Gateshead livery.

TRAMS and BUSES

Gateshead 10 was built by the Gateshead and District Tramways Company in 1925. It worked on routes in Gateshead and across the Tyne Bridge into Newcastle and Gosforth. Gateshead abandoned its tramway system in 1951. This tram was sold to British Railways to work on the electric railways between Grimsby and Immingham, where it stayed in service until 1961. Gateshead 10 has been repainted in the original maroon and cream of the Gateshead livery, and has seats for forty-eight passengers.

The oldest vehicle is Blackpool 31, which dates from 1901 and was built by the Midland Railway Carriage and Wagon Company. It was rebuilt in 1918 and stayed in passenger service with Blackpool Corporation Tramways until 1934. It was then transferred to the Engineering Department. The tram stayed in use until 1984, when it was moved to Beamish and restored to its former glory. It seats eighty-six passengers.

The smallest tram in service came from Oporto in Portugal. This class of tram was made in the 1930s to a pre-First World War design. The tram has been painted in the maroon and cream of the Gateshead livery.

Sheffield 264 dates from 1907, and was built by the United Electric Car Company of Preston for Sheffield Corporation Tramways. It stayed in service until 1956. Sheffield 264 has seats for fifty-nine passengers.

The Street is typical of a small North-East market town in 1913, and illustrates the development of trade and commerce.

The stables behind the Sun Inn house the dray horses of Newcastle Breweries. Before petrol and diesel engined vehicles became common, deliveries were made by horse-drawn drays. The horses are exercised daily in and around the town and museum. The tack room in the stables contains a fine collection of harness.

The Sun Inn was brought from High Bondgate in Bishop Auckland. It has been rebuilt with its original bar and select room, and is operated by Newcastle Breweries as a working pub, albeit at modern prices. The pub was a place for men. Respectable women did not visit public houses. Drinking was condoned by many employers. They argued that, if a man drank, he had good reason to earn money and so would be a good worker. Other employers, convinced by the arguments of the Methodists and Temperance Societies, discouraged drinking.

the TOWN

The park is a fine example of the amenities provided by local district and borough councils. Carefully tended flower beds, mown lawns, decorative cast iron railings and a drinking fountain, make it clear that this is a place for orderly recreation.

The bandstand was brought from Saltwell Park in Gateshead. Most communities and many collieries and factories had their own brass or silver bands. This tradition continues.
The successors of these bands play at Beamish on some Sunday afternoons in summer.

Many visitors to Beamish still quote to our staff the *'divi numbers'* of their parents and relatives.

The hardware department sold household appliances like mangles, possers and stoves, plus a wide range of domestic items for cleaning, repairing and improving the household. In the days before work tools were provided by employers, the Co-op also sold picks, shovels, *'bait'* tins and lamps.
To guarantee quality many of these items were manufactured in the Co-op's own factories, some of which, like Pelaw, were in the North East. Advertisements for these products can be seen on the shop walls. The drapery department sold everything from pit hoggers, (the traditional pitman's short trousers), to liberty bodices and corsets. For those who found made-up clothing expensive, the store sold materials, fabrics, threads, buttons, pins and needles.

The Co-op Store in the town street was once the central premises of the nearby Annfield Plain Industrial Co-operative Society, which dates back to 1873. It houses hardware, grocery and drapery departments plus the office of the Co-operative Insurance Society. The shops are stocked with goods available in a typical store of 1913. Above the heads of customers runs an original Lamson-Paragon cash system. This connects each department with the central cash office.

People were often suspicious of shop-keepers. Food was not always of good quality and was frequently adulterated. Customers believed that shop-keepers made excessive profits. The Co-operative movement was founded to allay these fears, and to direct profits back to its own members. Four times a year it paid a dividend, a percentage of the amount spent in the previous quarter. The *'divi'* was an important element in family house-keeping.

The grocery department shows a range of the foodstuffs available in 1913. In the days before home refrigeration or freezing, food was fresh, bottled, dried or canned. Dry goods were weighed by hand and carefully wrapped in different coloured paper bags; sugar in blue paper, lentils in yellow and raisins in purple. Small items were sold in paper cones. The Co-op had its own farms and dairies, and produced its own brands to guarantee purity and quality.

the cradle to the grave

the SOLICITOR

Opposite the park is a row of six terraced houses, part of a street of twenty-five homes, which once formed Ravensworth Terrace in Gateshead.

They were built between 1830 and 1845, and were originally the houses for fairly well-to-do tradesmen and professional people.

Cole & Son (Wallpapers) Ltd. No. PR 15230

Number 5 is a solicitor's office. The brass plaque on the front door proclaims the name of the practice, J. & R.S. Watson. Robert Spence Watson was a Quaker solicitor in Newcastle upon Tyne, and a prominent figure in national politics, education and industrial law. The main office at the front includes a fine partner's desk. The small standing desk was used by the solicitor when acting as the registrar of births, marriages and deaths.
The deed boxes are emblazoned with the names of prominent local families. Then, as now, the legal profession was conservative. This office, as well as the rear clerks' office, is still lit by gas lamps.

The general office has a Dickensian feel, with its high desks and stacks of letters, ledgers, plans and papers tied up with pink ribbon and red tape.

the MUSIC TEACHER

Number 2 Ravensworth Terrace is the house of an elderly music teacher, Miss Florence Smith. The house is furnished and decorated with fittings inherited from her parents. Unlike more affluent neighbours, the house has no running hot water or bathroom.

In 1913 there were few occupations available to middle class women. A single woman without private means could find herself in financial difficulties. The old age pension had recently been introduced, and was available only to people over seventy years of age.

People without inherited money or savings continued to work in order to avoid the disgrace of the workhouse.

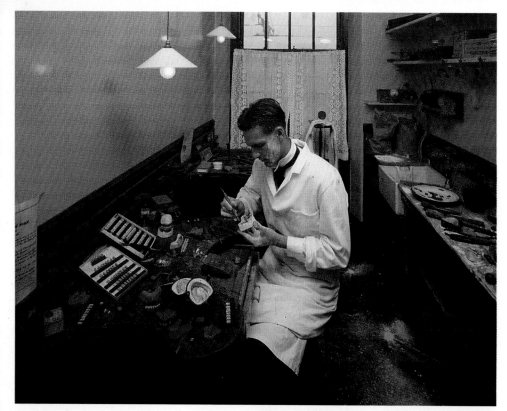

Numbers 3 and 4 Ravensworth Terrace are occupied by the dentist and his family. One house has been fitted out as a waiting room, surgery, recovery room and technician's workshop.

Like all medical treatment in the early years of this century, dental care was expensive.

Extractions were often done in street markets by untrained pullers of teeth. Until 1921 this was legal as long as the practitioner did not use the word dentist. Only the well-off could afford a visit to the dental surgery. A single filling could cost the equivalent of a week's wage for a working man. A set of false dentures, made of vulcanised rubber and porcelain, could cost several month's wages.

The surgery has an air of comfortable respectability. Though the equipment was sterilised daily, the treatment room, with its carpets, curtains and open fire, is far from antiseptic. The basic surgical equipment of today has changed little since 1913. Electric drills have since replaced the foot operated equipment which was slower.

Anaesthetic gas, (nitrous oxide or 'laughing gas'), was available to allay fears of pain for those prepared to pay extra.

An upstairs corridor leads to the dentist's elegantly furnished home. The house has an upstairs bath, shower and a flushing toilet. The master bedroom has a fashionable brass bed, and the nursery, at the sunny front of the house is furnished with cheerful prints and a wide range of toys.

the DENTIST

The dentist's wife had a servant to assist in the running of the household. The kitchen has both a well-polished range and a collection of new gadgets, including a vacuum cleaner and gas cooker. The Welsh dresser displays a fashionable dinner service. The servant's room in the attic was accessible only by a steep set of narrow stairs, and was lit by candles. This typical middle class family would have had two or three children. The space available for family life should be compared with the pit cottages where far larger families lived in less space and comfort.

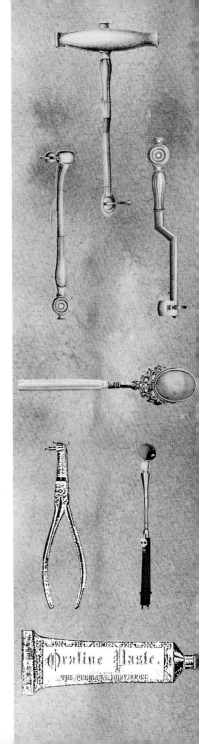

Oraline Paste.
THE PEERLESS DENTIFRICE

Opposite the Co-operative shops is the printer and stationer. The print shop upstairs represents the branch office of a local newspaper. Linotype machines and high speed automatic presses produced newspapers and periodicals. These were sent to branch offices for distribution. For small runs and proofing the nineteenth-century Columbian Eagle press or the Wharfdale Flat Bed press were still being used. The printer also produced business cards, stationery and advertising material for local companies. Though the telegraph and telephone system was being developed most business communication was still by mail and a large quantity of stationery was required.

In the ground floor stationery shop can be seen a wide range of paper goods, pens, pencils and office material of the period. Visitors can purchase reproductions of Victorian and Edwardian stationery.

the NEWSPAPER OFFICE

In the North East, coal was transported on wagonways or railways. The Stockton and Darlington railway was built in 1825. By 1880 the North Eastern Railway Company owned an extensive network of lines covering Northumberland, Durham and North Yorkshire. Many small railway lines have since closed. Some redundant station buildings have been brought to Beamish from all over the region.

The passenger station building is from Rowley, a hamlet on the A68 near Consett. The station was built in 1867.
It never had gas or electricity and was always lit by oil lamps. The cast iron footbridge leading to the goods yard is of a standard NER design dating from the 1870s, and was brought from Dunston.

The movement of trains was controlled by signalmen using hand operated frames of levers. The signalman was not allowed to leave his post during work hours on pain of instant dismissal. The signal box at Beamish was built in 1896, and originally stood at Carr House East, Consett.

The wrought iron footbridge leading from the station to the town was brought from Howden-le-Wear, Crook. The station area has been reconstructed to show a typical station on a branchline of the North Eastern Railway in 1913.

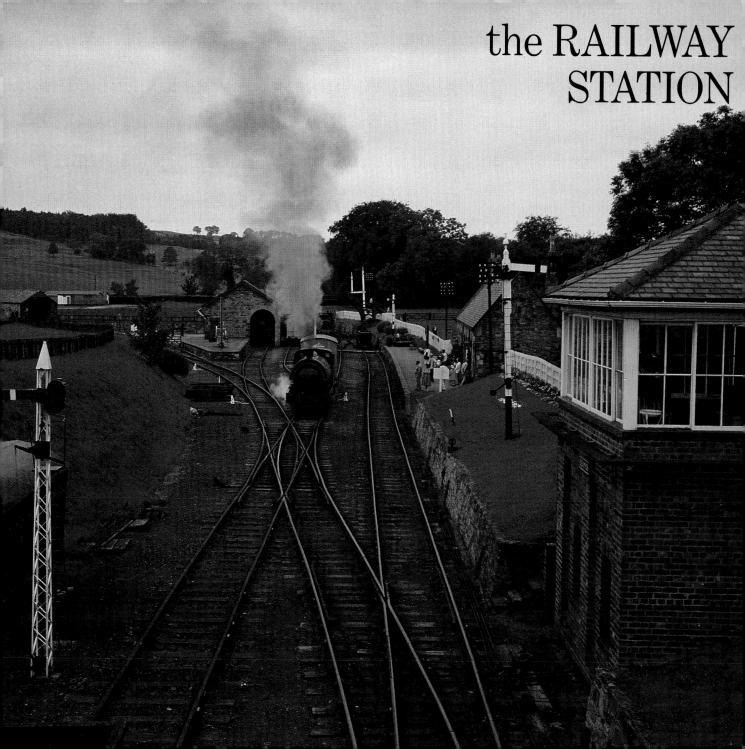

the RAILWAY STATION

the STATION YARD

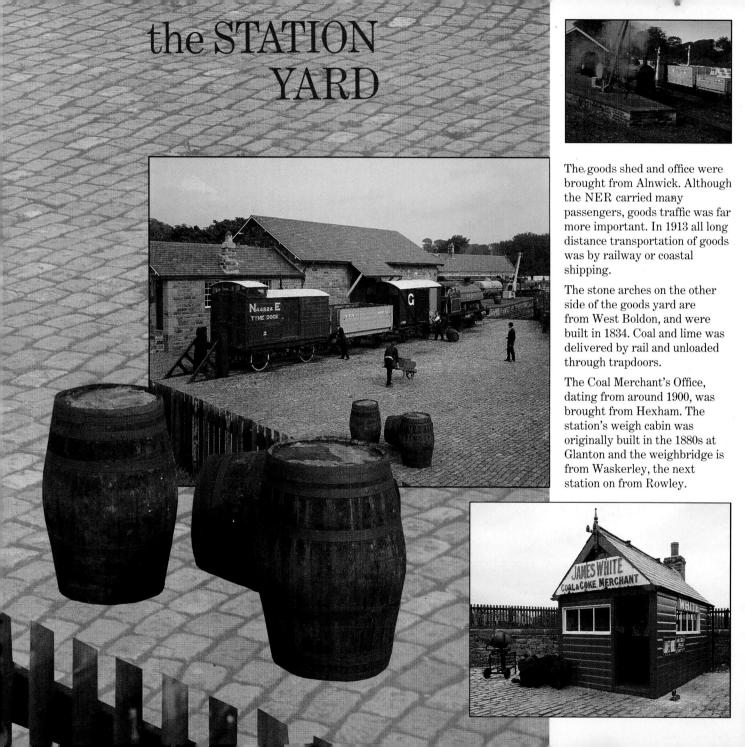

The goods shed and office were brought from Alnwick. Although the NER carried many passengers, goods traffic was far more important. In 1913 all long distance transportation of goods was by railway or coastal shipping.

The stone arches on the other side of the goods yard are from West Boldon, and were built in 1834. Coal and lime was delivered by rail and unloaded through trapdoors.

The Coal Merchant's Office, dating from around 1900, was brought from Hexham. The station's weigh cabin was originally built in the 1880s at Glanton and the weighbridge is from Waskerley, the next station on from Rowley.

No.14 0-4-0 Saddle Tank

Built in 1914 by Hawthorn Leslie for the Lambton and Hetton Collieries this locomotive was originally used for shunting duties in the yards of the Lambton and Hetton Collieries. In summer No.14 is in steam during part of the week, and is also used to haul the passenger service.

NER Class C1 No. 876 0-6-0 Tender Locomotive

This locomotive was built at the Gateshead works in 1889 for the North Eastern Railway. Two hundred and one engines of this class were eventually built as mixed traffic locomotives for use on branch lines. No 876 was in use until 1963, when it was withdrawn from service by British Railways. It is the last surviving locomotive in its class, and is currently awaiting a boiler refit and the rebuilding of its tender.

Visitors may find locomotives working in the station and colliery areas.

NER Luggage Composite Carriage No. 818

This carriage was built at the NER's York Carriage Works in 1903. It is 52ft. long, with three first-class and four third-class compartments, which are lit by gas. There is no corridor. Each compartment has its own door for passengers.

Locomotion No.1 0-4-0 Tender Locomotive

The original *Locomotion* was built by George Stephenson in 1825 for the Stockton and Darlington Railway. Like all early steam engines, each part had to be hand made. No standard specifications for engineering parts, such as screw threads, yet existed. This working replica was built by local engineering firms for the 150th Anniversary of the Stockton and Darlington Railway. *Locomotion* is often on loan to other museums around the world.

Twizell No.3 0-6-0 Side Tank

Built in 1891 by Robert Stephenson and Company for Lord Joicey's Beamish Wagonway, Twizell was in use until 1972. Similar 0-6-0 Tank engines were used by all the mainline railway companies for mixed traffic on branchlines. This is how Twizell will be used at Beamish. After a boiler re-fit Twizell will be in steam during the summer months.

the FAIRGROUND

The events field is the home of the fairground. The centrepiece is a restored carousel with galloping horses and strutting cockerels. This was originally owned by the Walkers, a well known fairground family. The traditional rides and attractions include swing boats, (known as *shuggy* boats in this region), flying chairs and a coconut shy.

As well as the central displays which remain constant, Beamish also organises special events throughout the year. The Friends of Beamish Museum organise three rallies for transport enthusiasts. The bicycle rally takes place in April, the Reliability Run, for vintage and veteran cars, in June, and the Trophy Trial, for veteran motor-cycles and tricycles, in September. Other events are organised for special weekends. These include the World Quoits Championship, north-country wrestling, whippet racing, car meets by devotees of Morgan, M.G. and Morris Minor cars, and quilting weekends.

Agricultural events include sheep clipping, the Shorthorn Show and a traditional Leek Show. The events are highlighted in the press and featured on the information board at the Entrance Building.

HOME FARM

Home Farm is a model farm and laid out in a typical Georgian pattern. It was owned by the Beamish estate and managed by a bailiff. In the twentieth-century, the farmsteading was abandoned due to mining subsidence, and has been restored by the museum. The main land holding is now occupied by Beamish Golf Club.

Some buildings have been added to the original farmstead. The pigsty, with a henhouse above, provides warmth for the hens and, reputedly, protection from foxes. It dates from about 1800, and came from New Ridley Farm, Stocksfield. The long stone built cart shed and smithy of 1905 was originally at Longhirst Lane Farm, Morpeth.

The hemmel or cowshed, opposite the farm, is an early corrugated iron farm building. It dates from 1908, and was brought to Beamish from the original site at Corbridge. The stone hemmel, beside the duckpond, dates from around the 1790s, and comes from Acklington in Northumberland.

Farming is a business. Crops and stock are produced and sold for profit. Most farm animals were killed for meat or kept for wool, milk and eggs. They were also a source of leather, fats and grease for the growing industries of the North-East. By the early twentieth-century oxen, previously important providers of power, were obsolete.

Most of the work on northern farms was done with horses and they were also bred for sale to industry and collieries. The heavy horses you will see around the farm will be used for traditional horse-farming. Farm animals can be seen in different parts of the farm or in the fields. Their daily location depends upon the seasons and weather conditions. The cattle and sheep are from old established breeds that were common before the requirements of mass production led to specialisation.

Home Farm was acquired by the museum in 1972. The house was in a very delapidated state and has been restored. The stone fireplace in the kitchen dates from the 1700s. The kitchen range was manufactured around 1910, and was discovered in a local farm house.

The kitchen was the main room of the house and the centre of most household activity. Here the family and farmworkers gathered for meals around the large table. In the upland areas of the north, oats were a staple part of the diet and the drying rack, or flake, above the fireplace was used for drying oatcakes. The back kitchen was used as a washhouse and as a food preparation area.

It is equipped with a cooking range and a large copper pot for boiling clothes, linen and bedding. Although the farmhouse is large and well-fitted, farming was in decline in 1913. A visit to the Co-op demonstrates that much food was being imported from Holland, Denmark, America and the British Empire. Farmers were still relatively affluent. The pay of the farm labourers, however, compared badly with industrial workers and miners.

Blacksmiths were valued
members of the community.
They served long apprentice-
ships, and the craft was often
handed down from father to son.
They shoed horses and repaired
equipment. The village
blacksmith supplied everything
from pots and pans, to work
tools and toys, like the
traditional iron hoops or *boolers*.

The cattle at Beamish are the result of a careful breeding programme. They have been bred to produce the typical appearance of the Shorthorn cattle found on many northern farms at the beginning of the century.

The selective breeding of cattle to produce a *true* strain was formalised in the eighteenth-century. Herd books, formal records of animal pedigrees, started to be kept in the nine-teenth century. The Shorthorn was an all round beast, good both for milk and meat. It had a placid disposition. Some special beasts, as publicity for the breed, were transported long distances and were shown at fairs. One of the most famous, The Durham Ox, gave his name to public houses all over Britain. Paintings and prints of famous Shorthorn cattle can be seen on the walls of the farmhouse.

In the second half of the nineteenth-century traditional farming went into decline. The growth of the railways made it possible for fresh milk to be transported over long distances Dairy farming flourished. Small producers in less accessible areas still specialised in local cheese and butter but cheap imported cheese threatened traditional markets.

Cheesemaking is shown at Beamish. In the dairy we make the traditional semi-hard cheeses of the northern dales. It is available for sale to museum visitors, and is also available in selected food shops in the region.

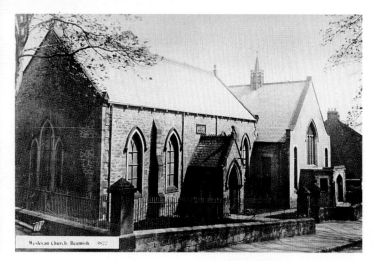
Wesleyan Church, Beamish. 1822.

the CHAPEL and SCHOOL

The Wesleyan Methodist Chapel stood originally in Beamish village. Non-conformists, were especially strong in this region. Newcastle upon Tyne was one of the first areas to support the teachings of John and Charles Wesley. Methodists were drawn from the working class, shipworkers, miners, shop assistants, farm and factory workers and their families.

The chapel at Pit Hill was first built in 1854, and had to be extended in order to cope with increased congregations. Sunday services were held each morning and evening. The whole week was filled with activity, both social and spiritual.

PREPARE TO MEET THY GOD.

In 1913 the chapel had a thriving Women's Bright Hour, a class meeting for bible study, a Band of Hope temperance meeting and an active choir and musical group. The Boys' Brigade, Girls' Brigade, Young Rechabites and Sunday School ministered to the young.

Chapels were efficiently organised. The proper conduct of meetings, and the keeping of minutes and accounts, provided important training for the early Labour Party and trade unions. Chapel folk were prominent in supporting home and foreign missions, and in organising charity and hospital work.

Next to the chapel, Beamish is rebuilding a Victorian school from nearby East Stanley. This first opened in 1892 and was the first Board school in the town. By 1913, the school was well established, providing a basic elementary education. Teaching centred on the three R's. Children learned by rote, chanting multiplication tables and reciting poetry. Wall maps and charts illustrated history and geography lessons, and general knowledge was taught in object lessons.

Some children won scholarships to higher grade schools, but not all were able to continue their education. Most left at thirteen years of age. Some, those clever enough to pass reading and arithmetic tests, left earlier to start work and contribute to the family budget.

the PIT COTTAGES

The North East was built on coal. Once the region was dominated by pits and pit villages.

In 1913, most pitmen lived in houses owned by colliery companies. This row of cottages was brought to the Museum from Francis Street, Hetton-le-Hole, County Durham. They were part of a row of twenty-seven houses built by the Hetton Coal Company in the 1860s, and were lived in by pitmen's families until 1976.

The cottages are shown as they would have appeared just before the First World War. Pitmen had a taste for solid furniture and substantial decoration. Family life centred on the two downstairs rooms, particularly the kitchen. Oil lamps and candles supplied light. Coal was provided free. The kitchen range included a coal-fired oven and a water heater. A single tap in the pantry provided cold water. There was no bathroom. A tin bath in front of the kitchen range was usual. Each cottage had an outside netty, or earth closet.

In pit villages women married young and bore large numbers of children at home. They had thus little opportunity for paid work. Keeping the home, washing, cleaning, baking and feeding the family was a full time and onerous task.

The long gardens were a source of food and recreation. Pitmen were keen gardeners. They grew vegetables and bred poultry and rabbits for the pot. Byelaws forbade keeping pigs close to houses. Leek growing, pigeon fancying and whippet racing were popular pastimes, a ready excuse for gambling.

No. 1 Francis Street is shown as a colliery office, a common practice at smaller pits. The general office, where pitmen were paid once a fortnight, is situated at the back. The front office is where the manager, a qualified mining engineer, was based.

Nos. 2, 3 and 4 show the homes of typical pit families. They illustrate the influence of both the Methodists and the Catholic Church in mining communities. No. 5 Francis Street is fitted out for use by school children on special educational projects.

Behind the cottages is a collection of sheds or crees. These were constructed by the pitmen from old timber, metal signs and window frames, and were used as basic but effective workshops, greenhouses and stores.

the DRIFT MINE

The Colliery yard contains both the entrance to Mahogany Drift and the pit headgear of a deep mine. A drift mine is a tunnel driven into coal seams which lie near to the surface. Mahogany Drift was here long before the museum, and was worked for over a hundred years from the 1850s to 1958. It has now been partially re-opened for visitors who are given guided tours underground.

Pitmen had special names for the tools and techniques they used. Mahogany Drift was worked by the pillar and stall method. Tunnels, known as roads, were dug horizontally into seams of coal. Smaller side tunnels were then dug. Pillars of coal were left to support the roof. Hewers cut the coal by hand, sometimes using tools powered by compressed air. They worked an eight hour shift of hard physical labour in difficult, often wet, conditions. They ate their food, known as bait, underground.

The coal was shovelled into tubs which were pushed to the road. They were then pulled by pit ponies and mechanical haulage to the surface. Moving tubs was the task of boys, often as young as fourteen years of age. They were known as putters and pony putters. The hewers were paid for the tonnage of coal they cut, the putters by the total of tubs they moved. By the standards of 1913, most miners were well paid. A hewer could expect to earn 38 shillings a week (£1.90p), a putter 35 shillings (£1.75p), and a pony putter 12s.6d. (63p).

Underground, the pitmen were under the control of the Deputy, who was responsible for the output and the safety of his district. He was identified by a leather helmet and carried a wand, or yardstick, to measure the distance between the wooden pit props which held up the roof.

Mines were dangerous places to work. Accidents were frequent and disasters, common. An underground explosion, in 1909 at West Stanley, killed one hundred and sixty-eight miners. Sixty of these were boys.

Once mined, coal had to be brought to the surface. In mines the tubs would be pulled along on an endless rope or by a main and tail hauler. In deep pits the tubs were loaded into cages which were brought up the shaft by the winding engine. The large wheels of the tall headstock were a distinctive feature of collieries.

The winding engine at Beamish was used at Beamish No. 2 pit from 1855. Attached to the stone winding engine house is the wooden heapstead, and the screens building from Ravensworth Park in Gateshead.

Coal was weighed, sorted and picked over in these buildings before being loaded into railway wagons. The engineman operated the winding engine. The banksman operated the cages. The checkweighman weighed the coal tubs. They were all well paid because of the responsibility of their jobs.

The screens were extremely dirty and noisy places to work. Boys would work here alongside men who had been injured or were too old to work underground. Surface men worked ten or twelve hour shifts but were paid less per week than underground workers.

the COLLIERY

The pit heap was formed from stone and waste tipped from tubs pushed along the gantry. Pit heaps often caught fire and burnt for long periods.

Coal was transported from the collieries by railway. The large colliery combines ran their own railway systems. Some collieries used traditional chaldron wagons. Others used wagons resembling those of the North Eastern Railway. Most collieries had a locomotive shed where the shunting engine was kept and maintained.

Hetton is one of the oldest locomotives in the world. It was built in 1822 by George Stephenson. Hetton worked until 1912, and was last steamed at the 1925 Stockton & Darlington Railway centenary celebrations.

This Brief Guide is one of a series planned publications.
In preparation are books on the history of the museum, chapel life, schools and shopping.
Future books will cover colliery life, transport, public health, politics, trade unionists etc.

This guide has been produced by Derek Harris, Jim Lawson & Jon Price under the editorship of the Museum Director, Peter Lewis. It was designed by Jackie Baines of the Robin Wade & Pat Read Design Partnership and printed in England by Smith Print Group Ltd.
ISBN 0 905054 067

Photographs by Eddie Ryle-Hodges and Peter Richardson
Additional material from Tommy Thompson

BRINGING YOU ALL THE NORTH EAST
∘∘ NEWS FOR OVER A CENTURY ∘∘

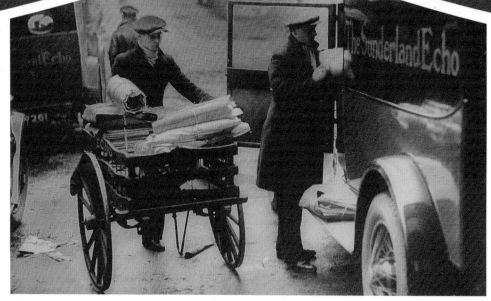

The Sunderland Echo

The first copy of The Sunderland Echo was printed on December 22 1873, on a flatbed press in Press Lane, Sunderland. Mr. Samuel Storey, future Mayor and M.P. for Sunderland, and Chairman of Durham County Council, founded the paper with six partners to fill a gap in the life of the town. Mr. Storey wrote the first comment column for the Echo in which he promised that if things were wrong the Echo would do its best to put them right, but "always with moderation and without esteeming all who oppose us as fools and knaves...... Our aim will be to afford generous support to friends and exercise forbearance towards foes". Since then the Echo has sought to maintain that high principle.

The Hartlepool Mail

The Hartlepool Mail was originally a weekly, the successor to several ill-fated publications. The first issue of the Mail's predecessor, The South Durham Herald, came out on May 26, 1866. Foreign affairs were the immediate cause of the decision to go daily and The Hartlepool Mail was born in 1877. In 1883 the title was changed to The Northern Daily Mail and in 1884 the three papers, The Herald, The Mail and The Stockton Journal were bought by the Carnegie - Storey Newspaper Syndicate. After the syndicate broke up, Mr. Storey retained newspapers in Hartlepool, Sunderland and Portsmouth. Portsmouth and Sunderland Newspapers Limited was formed in 1934.

Registered Head Office: The Echo, Pennywell, Sunderland SR4 9ER